Koalas

A U S T R A L I A

Steve Parish

DISCOVERING AUSTRALIAN KOALAS

Why is the Koala so appealing? It appears to be a living teddy bear, designed to cling and be cuddled. However, this soft-furred all-Australian animal is far more interesting than any toy. It is wonderfully adapted to its tough environment, and its family life and social interactions are fascinating.

It is difficult for a human to comprehend the Koala's lifestyle. For one thing, it lives in trees and seldom comes to the ground. Also, its diet is limited to the leaves of a limited number of gum tree, or eucalypt, species. Eucalypt leaves are wax covered, full of fibre and pungent with oils and other, sometimes toxic, substances. They are low in nutrients and supply little energy, so the Koala spends much of its time sleeping or dozing. When a Koala eventually awakes, it usually sets about eating still more gum leaves.

Opposite:
A Koala's two thumbs help it hold branches firmly.

WHERE CAN I SEE A KOALA?

Spotting a wild Koala in the bush can be a thrilling experience. A rounded shape perched in the fork of a tree, or clinging to a trunk, may be revealed as one of the bushland's most elusive creatures. Koalas do not flee and hide from observers, but they are camouflaged by their bark-coloured fur and daytime immobility.

Koalas are found in coastal, lowland, eucalypt forests, usually near watercourses, from Queensland to Victoria. A few groups exist in South Australia, there is a colony on Kangaroo Island and groups may be seen in zoos, sanctuaries and wildlife refuges such as the one on Victoria's Phillip Island.

A number of zoos and wildlife parks provide breeding and display facilities for this precious element of Australia's native fauna, and individuals from overcrowded habitats may be relocated to more remote bushlands.

Opposite:
A Koala is camouflaged by its colour and its immobility.

4

THE KOALA AT HOME

Koalas and eucalypt trees are inseparable. In southern Australia, Koalas are most often found in manna gum, while in Queensland their favourite food is the leaf of the forest red gum. They may browse on up to fifteen other sorts of trees, including southern blue gum, Sydney blue gum, messmate, stringy-bark, swamp gum, tallowwood, grey gum and flooded gum.

Koalas from the cooler southern areas of Australia usually have much longer coats and are heavier than those from Queensland. They need the extra fur to keep them warm because Koalas do not build nests but endure all sorts of weather sitting in their treetop home.

Opposite:
Long-furred
southern Koala

Right:
Koala habitat

AN AGILE CLIMBER

There is little danger of a Koala falling from its tree. Its stub of a tail allows it to sit firmly against a branch, clinging with long, strong arms and legs. Each of a Koala's forepaws has two thumbs, all four paws have roughened pads, and the digits end in sharp, strong, curved claws.

On the ground, a Koala bounds on all fours at some speed, but is vulnerable to predators and falls easy prey to dogs if intercepted when moving between trees.

Opposite and left: A tiny, stubby tail makes it easy for a Koala to sit propped on a sloping branch.

THE KOALA'S DIET

Each year, eucalypt trees bear fragrant masses of ballerina-skirted blossoms. The flowers attract possums, flying-foxes, insects and a variety of nectar-eating birds, which carry their pollen from one bouquet to the next. The Koala, however, ignores the floral beauty, preferring to munch on leaves.

The Koala's distant ancestors lived in the rainforests, long ago when Australia was a much wetter place. During the millions of years in which the continent grew drier, the Koala adapted to browse on the leaves of the drought-resistant eucalypts that replaced the rainforests.

Opposite:
Selecting a
leaf to eat

Right:
Eucalypt
blossoms

DINING IN THE TREETOPS

A Koala carefully inspects a selection of gum leaves before placing them one by one into its mouth, grinding them up with its molar teeth and swallowing. Some leaves, possibly those containing high levels of toxic substances, are rejected. The Koala's liver will get rid of the poisons that remain.

The Koala has a very long caecum (the human equivalent of this organ is the appendix). It contains tiny organisms which ferment the leaves and make the sugars and starches they contain available for use.

The Koala's placid lifestyle is a result of its restricted diet, which is very low in energy-producing substances. It may sleep 19 hours of each 24, and rarely needs to drink because eucalypt leaves contain water levels of up to 50%.

Opposite:
A Koala reaches for a sprig of leaves, displaying its strong, clawed digits and two thumbs.

Left:
Koala habitat

KOALA SURVIVAL

Clearing of eucalypt forests still threatens Koalas. Unfortunately, the best Koala habitat is fertile land along watercourses – just the environment humans need for their own living space.

Other threats to the furry tree-dwellers are fire, dogs, motor vehicles and disease that can cause infertility. Disease strikes where too many Koalas become crowded into refuge habitats.

Koalas are great favourites with Australians and visitors to Australia, and there is awareness that, while they are relatively plentiful now, it would not take much to unbalance their numbers.

Although there are Koalas in wildlife parks, the species is healthiest if wild populations are maintained. With careful management, Koalas will go on as unique creatures of the Australian bush.

Opposite:
Koalas were
once seen as
sources of fur.

Opposite:
Pulling down a
spray of leaves

Left:
Selecting the
perfect leaf

KOALA BABIES

Koalas live in home ranges that may be no larger than 3 ha, and in the spring and summer breeding season both males and females travel on the ground between clumps of trees to find mates. The strongest male in an area mates with most of the local females in a breeding season. Thirty-five days after mating, a female gives birth to a tiny, naked, blind joey, which hauls itself into her pouch and fastens onto a nipple. It will not emerge for around 6 months, and will not be weaned until one year of age. Then it will stay with its mother for another year before wandering away.

Opposite:
A joey this age will not wander far from its mother.

Left:
A young Koala will cling to its mother's back.

REARING YOUNG

After first leaving the pouch, a young Koala clings to its mother's back as she moves about, or sleeps lying across her lap. It pushes its head into her pouch to suckle, or investigates the gum leaves on which she is feeding. After it leaves the pouch for good, at about 8 months of age, it grows rapidly, its teeth emerge and it begins to eat leaves.

Opposite and right:
A young Koala grows rapidly, and soon starts to investigate its world.

WEANING

Before a young Koala can digest eucalypt leaves, it must acquire the micro-organisms that its digestive system will need in order to break down the fibre they contain. At this stage, it eats special, soft droppings produced by its mother and so takes in the necessary micro-organisms.

A young female will probably eat much the same diet as its mother did, but a young male, forced to wander further to find a home range, may be forced to experiment with new sorts of leaves not available in its original home.

Opposite and left: A young Koala is entirely dependent on its mother.

LEARNING TO BE A KOALA

A young Koala may benefit from watching its mother carefully choose the best eucalypt leaves to eat. Certainly an adult Koala spends considerable time sniffing a spray of leaves before munching the first one, and it has excellent reasons for doing so. Eucalypt leaves normally contain toxic substances, oils and tannins, and at certain times some leaves are too high in these components for even a Koala to swallow.

Opposite:
This Koala keeps a safe grip on a branch with its foot while pulling down leaves.

Left:
Selecting a leaf to eat

LORD OF THE BRANCHES

Eventually, a young male Koala leaves his mother's area of bush and sets off to find his own home range. He will be driven away by older males defending their territories, but sooner or later will claim a group of trees as his own. He will mark these trees by rubbing them with an orange fluid produced by scent glands on his chest.

He advertises his presence by bellowing loudly and may fight another male fiercely for the privilege of mating with a receptive female.

Opposite:
The patch on a male Koala's chest marks the opening to scent glands.

Left:
A male Koala prepares to mark his territory.